HOW
DO I
BECOME
AN . . . ?

ARCHITECT

Mindi Rose Englart

Photographs by Peter Casolino

BLACKBIRCH®
PRESS

THOMSON
GALE

San Diego • Detroit • New York • San Francisco • Cleveland • New Haven, Conn. • Waterville, Maine • London • Munich

For more information, contact
The Gale Group, Inc.
27500 Drake Rd.
Farmington Hills, MI 48331-3535
Or you can visit our Internet site at http://www.gale.com

Photo Credits: Cover, all photos © Peter Casolino; except pages 13, 18, 27, 31 © Woodruff/Brown Photography for Svigals & Partners

LIBRARY OF CONGRESS CATALOGING-IN-PUBLICATION DATA

Englart, Mindi.
  Architect / by Mindi Rose Englart.
    v. cm. — (How do I become a: series)
  Summary: Examines the role of the architect, including educational requirements, the development of designs, and working with clients, contractors, and consultants.
    ISBN 1-56711-686-8
  1. Architects—Vocational guidance—Juvenile literature. [1. Architects—Vocational guidance. 2. Vocational guidance.] I. Title. II. Series.
  NA1995 .E54 2003
  720'.92—dc21   2002005376

Printed in China
10 9 8 7 6 5 4 3 2

Contents

Dedication
To my friends in my favorite building—the one with the courtyard.

Special Thanks
The publisher and the author would like to thank Jay Brotman, Barry Svigals, Margaret Bailey, and the Svigals + Partners staff, as well John Jacobson and Louise Hartman of the Yale University Architecture School, for their generous help in putting this project together.

There are about 90,000 licensed architects in the United States today. In fact, an architect probably designed your home! Architects are trained in the art and science of building design. To become architects, students study drawing, math, and science in college. There is also an artistic side to being an architect. An architect must care how other people feel when they are in the buildings he or she designs.

How does someone learn to be an architect?

An architect with his drawings ▶

3

Architecture School

There are two ways for people to become architects. High school graduates can go on to earn a five-year bachelor of architecture degree at a college. Students may also attend four years of college and then continue for another two years to get a master of architecture degree.

In school, students learn about the history of architecture. They see pictures of well-known buildings from different periods in history. For example, students may study the pyramids at Giza, Egypt, which were built around 2600 B.C. Teachers will point out important facts about the pyramids. They explain what materials were used to build them, what they were used for, and how they were built. Students look at famous buildings to get ideas for their own designs.

◀ **The pyramids at Giza, Egypt**

Students study ▶ design together.

In the Classroom

Architecture students must use math and science to design buildings that will be safe and will last a long time. Students take algebra, geometry, and calculus classes. A math formula can be used to figure out how much weight a certain type of steel can hold. Another formula can tell an architect how many bricks it will take to build his or her design. This kind of information helps architects make smart choices as they work to turn an idea into a real building.

Students also take physics courses. They learn how to design a structure that will withstand the forces of gravity, wind, and earthquakes. They also take classes to learn how to build with different materials, including wood, metal, and concrete.

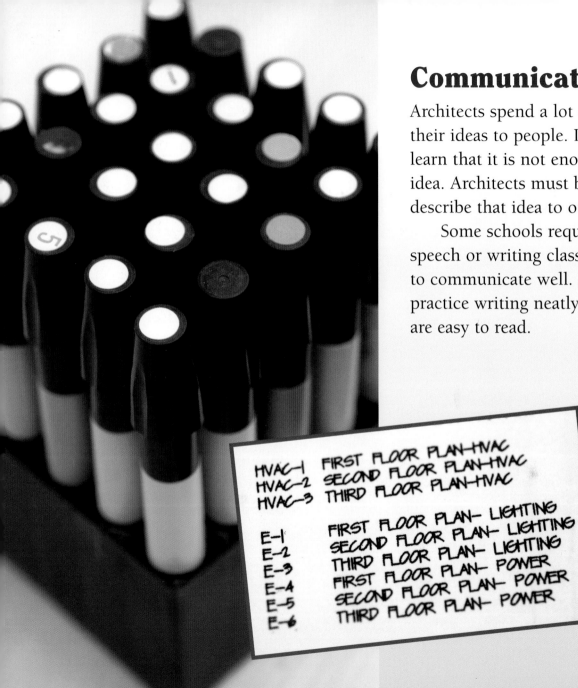

Communicating Ideas

Architects spend a lot of time explaining their ideas to people. In school, students learn that it is not enough to have a good idea. Architects must be able to clearly describe that idea to others.

Some schools require students to take speech or writing classes to help them to communicate well. Architects even practice writing neatly so their instructions are easy to read.

HVAC–1   FIRST FLOOR PLAN–HVAC
HVAC–2   SECOND FLOOR PLAN–HVAC
HVAC–3   THIRD FLOOR PLAN–HVAC

E–1   FIRST FLOOR PLAN– LIGHTING
E–2   SECOND FLOOR PLAN– LIGHTING
E–3   THIRD FLOOR PLAN– LIGHTING
E–4   FIRST FLOOR PLAN– POWER
E–5   SECOND FLOOR PLAN– POWER
E–6   THIRD FLOOR PLAN– POWER

◀ Architects need to have neat handwriting.

Schools also teach students to communicate through their drawings. Students use pencil, ink, and markers to sketch building plans. Students also learn to use special computer programs to draw building designs on computer screens. These programs are called CADD (computer-aided design and drafting) programs. CADD programs allow architects to create and print precise drawings of their designs. These designs show every detail of a building design.

▼ An architect uses a CADD program to create a design.

Students work ▲
at drafting tables.

Building a model ▶

8

Design Studio

At the beginning of the school year, each student is assigned a studio. In their studios, students work alone, or in groups, to create sample building projects. Students draw designs and build models to show their ideas to classmates and teachers. They use different materials to build their models, such as cardboard, cotton balls, wire, paint, and clay. Teachers visit the studios to give students advice about their work.

A professor looks at a student's work. ▶

Critiques

Students present their work to their teacher and fellow students. This is called a critique. It is important because it lets a student hear how his or her design looks to others. A student may not have thought of everything to include in a drawing or model. A teacher or fellow student may point out that something is missing. For example, a teacher may explain that if a building will be in a cold climate, it will need to be made of a material that holds in heat, such as brick. The student can use this critique to improve the design.

Students listen to a critique. ▼

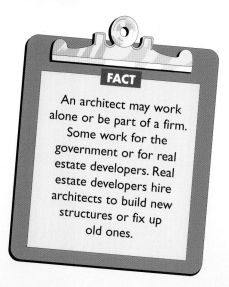

▲ **An internship is a form of on-the-job training.**

Internship

An internship is on-the-job training. Interns work at an architecture firm, which is a business that hires architects. Interns are paid to do work, but they are supervised by an experienced architect. Internships allow architects to practice what they have learned in school. This work experience is part of an architect's training. Interns can ask the boss lots of questions.

Interns learn from experienced architects. They help licensed architects create building plans. They may create construction drawings on CADD, build models, or help to design a project. Interns also use this time to prepare for the Architect Registration Examination.

The Architect Registration Examination

Architects must be licensed. This proves that they have the knowledge and experience to build safe buildings. It usually takes about eight to ten years to become a licensed architect. Architects must pass the ARE (Architect Registration Examination) to become licensed.

The ARE tests architects on their knowledge of the field of architecture. It tests to see how well they can draft, or draw, plans. Questions on the ARE test an architect's ability to work with others in related fields, such as engineers and carpenters.

Students must pass the ▶ ARE to become licensed.

The Architectural Firm

Svigals + Partners is an architectural firm in New Haven, Connecticut. Since 1983, Svigals + Partners has designed houses, schools, and science laboratories around the United States. Barry Svigals is an architect. He is also an artist. He creates sculptures that are included in the walls and staircases of many of his buildings.

◀ **The atrium of the Wallace E. Carroll School of Management at Boston College was designed by Svigals + Partners.**

Working with Clients

People, called clients, hire architects to design new buildings or to change existing ones. Sometimes a client is a family that wants a home built. A client may also be a company or a government agency. For example, a school board may want to add more space onto a school. Clients must be comfortable with the architect they hire.

When clients want to hire an architect, they send out a Request for Proposal (RFP). This asks the architect to describe his or her skills and experience. The firm then puts together a brochure for the client. This brochure has pictures and descriptions of the architect's past projects. Usually, they are similar to the building the client wants to build. It also includes the names, jobs, and work experience of all the people who will work on the project.

◀ **A manager prints out pages for the brochure.**

A client meets with the architect to discuss the new project. At this meeting, the architect asks questions. He or she tries to understand more about what the client wants. The architect and client look at models and pictures. They decide how to do the project.

Architects gather information about a project.

Research and Planning

Architects research the best ways to get a job done. There are many things to think about to make sure a project will turn out well. For example, an important part of an architect's job is to stay within a client's budget. This is the amount of money a client can spend. An architect finds out how much money it will cost to build a design. They then give this information to their client. They make sure the client is willing to spend that amount of money.

Architects also pay attention to studies that describe how people feel in and around buildings. Once an architect knows this kind of information, he or she can design the building according to a client's needs. For example, researchers have learned that children learn best in natural light, with windows that open, and with a flow of fresh air. Therefore, an architect may decide to design a school with lots of windows.

Schematics

After doing the necessary research, an architect comes up with creative designs for a client's building. An architect draws ideas. He or she shares them with engineers—and other architects— to get advice. These early drawings are called schematics.

Sometimes an architect designs a set of buildings—such as a college campus, or a theme park. They will draw up a master plan. This includes all of the buildings and the spaces in between them.

▼ **Architects revise their plans.**

17

Think Like an Architect

You can practice thinking like an architect wherever you go— at home, in school, or at a shopping center. Notice how light, colors, textures, spaces, and shapes make you feel. Look for light and dark, big and small, and old and new when you look at a building. If you learn to see how the settings work together to make you feel comfortable, you will be thinking like an architect.

◄ **Practice thinking like an architect in school.**

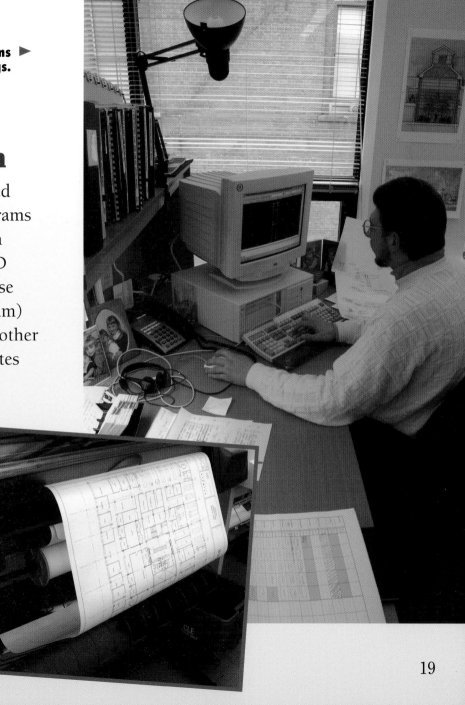

Computer Aided Drafting and Design

Most architects use Computer Aided Drafting and Design (CADD) programs to create schematics. Architects can make detailed drawings with CADD programs. For example, they can use AutoCAD (a popular CADD program) to draw buildings with curves and other special shapes. AutoCAD then creates measurements for each curve or shape. Builders use these measurements to construct buildings. CADD allows architects to easily add to a design or take parts away. This way, architects can test lots of design ideas before they decide on a final one.

Architects use a special printer to print very large drawings. ▶

19

The Design

Architects must choose materials that will last a long time. They consider things like the local weather and what the building will be used for. For example, a hospital will need to be designed differently than a pet store because they have different needs.

Architectural firms have a product library. Thousands of product samples are stored there. An architect can view samples of all kinds of building materials, such as bricks, wood, and plumbing parts.

Architectural teams meet often. They work on drawings and models. Architects look at models from different angles. They try to understand how people will feel when they are near or inside a building. Architects also meet with consultants. These people can be builders, engineers, or interior designers. They help an architect design a safe and sturdy building.

▲ **An architect looks at brick samples.**

An architect updates plans. ▶

21

Interior designers look at paint cards to choose a color.

Teamwork

An architect puts together a team of workers for each project. A team is made up of people who are trained to work on a construction project. Some projects require additional help. For example, a building in California may need a special engineer to make sure the building can withstand an earthquake. A veterinary clinic may need help from someone trained in animal care.

Architects often work with interior designers. Like architects, interior designers know that people are affected by colors and materials. They are careful to look at the style an architect has created in a plan. They select materials to go with the look of the design. Designers choose carpet samples, paint colors, furniture pieces, lights, and tiles. They must be creative. They also know how long most materials will last and how much they cost.

Matching tiles ▶ to a floor design

23

Model Buildings

Architectural models are important because they give a three-dimensional view of how the building will look. The architect uses cardboard, wood, or plastics to build a model. He or she also uses knives, glue, pencils, rulers, and paint. Architects sometimes add miniature trees and cars around model buildings. This helps to show the size of a building. It also shows how it will look with people and things around it.

An architect uses rulers and different knives to carefully score, or create lines, in cardboard. This makes a building look like it is made of wood or other materials.

Using a knife ▶ to cut cardboard

Project Manual

For every building, an architect must create a project manual. In this book, an architect makes schedules for the building contractor. The contractor is in charge of constructing an architect's designs. Schedules describe every part of a building. For example, each door is numbered and listed in the project manual. This way, a contractor can find the size of the door, the materials used to make the door, and even the kind of hinges and knobs used for the door. The contractor will also find mechanical, electrical, and plumbing information for the entire building.

Builders also use a book with a final set of drawings called construction documents. These two books have all of the information needed to construct a building.

FACT

People don't realize how much paperwork is needed to create a single building. Even things as small as nails are described in the project manual. This manual can be hundreds of pages long.

Renovations vs. New Construction

Sometimes architects design new buildings. Other times, they renovate, or rebuild, old buildings. Renovations can give an old building a new look. Another benefit to renovating is that leftover materials can be reused.

Sometimes part of a building will need to be demolished, or knocked down, for safety reasons. An architect may ask that some of the materials—such as bricks or pipes—be kept for use in a new addition. When architects add a new section onto an old building, they might ask for new bricks or other materials to be made to look older than they are. This way, new parts blend with old ones. Often, architects use building materials that are made nearby. Then they can support local businesses and save money on transportation costs. An architect may choose building materials that have been recycled if the building is renovated.

▲ **Some architects choose to renovate old buildings.**

◄ **An architect meets with a building contractor to discuss plans.**

The Building Site

Building contractors are in charge of the construction of buildings that architects design. An architect meets with a building contractor many times. They answer questions. They also check to see how the building is coming along.

Sometimes a contractor realizes that an architect's design needs to be changed. When this happens, the architect and the building contractor work together to solve the problem. They work to make safer choices and try to solve problems quickly.

A construction site ▶

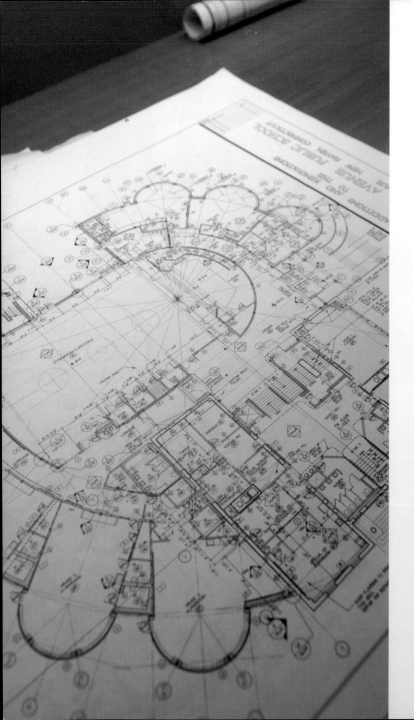

Grand Opening

A building can take years to finish. That is why its completion is so exciting! Often, there will be a grand opening ceremony to celebrate the event. A grand opening allows the people who will use the building to meet and celebrate with the people who designed and constructed it. Once a building has its grand opening, it's time for architects to start a new project.

◀ **Plans for the Edgewood Avenue K-8 Arts Magnet School in New Haven, Connecticut**

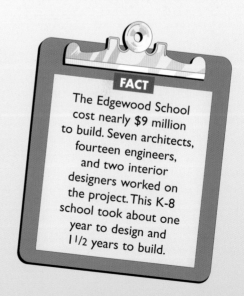

FACT

The Edgewood School cost nearly $9 million to build. Seven architects, fourteen engineers, and two interior designers worked on the project. This K-8 school took about one year to design and 1 1/2 years to build.

▲ Model for the Edgewood school

▲ The newly built Edgewood school

Glossary

Architecture The profession of designing and constructing buildings

Budget How much money a person can spend

Building contractor A professional who supervises the construction of buildings that architects design

CADD Computer Aided Drafting and Design

Consultant An experienced professional who offers their skills or advice to a project

Critiques A time when students can get feedback on their work

Design studio In architectural school, where students do their work

Intern A person who works with experienced professionals to learn a job

For More Information

Books

Miller, Jake. *On the Job with an Architect: Builder of the World*. Hauppage, NY: Barron's, Juveniles, 2001.

Website

Official website of Svigals + Partners

www.svigals.com

Index